I really wanted to go for a holiday to Far North Queensland. There are many interesting people and places there. Yarrabah Aboriginal mission is there. Yarrabah community is called a mission because the community was set up by Christian missionaries. In the old days the Aboriginal people went to missions to be protected from dangerous settlers. They were safer at the missions.

I needed to work to save money for the holiday. I worked very hard. The holiday was going to cost a lot of money. Money was needed for the flights, hire car, food, place to stay, and fun. After some time, I saved enough money for the big trip. I was now ready to plan my holiday.

One day I was talking to my friend from work about the holiday plan. My friend was very excited to hear about the holiday. He told me that his Dad is from Yarrabah. He told me his Dad is from a large family with many relatives in Yarrabah. He told me to visit his relatives and say “hello”. I was excited to visit the relatives of my workmate.

When I arrived in North Queensland it was very hot. Even though it was winter it was still hot. It was very green with lots of forests and beaches. I was scared to swim at the beaches. There are crocodiles in North Queensland. I made sure I was safe around the water. I am not worried to say, I am very scared of crocodiles. The people are used to living around crocodiles in North Queensland.

There were many Aboriginal and Torres Strait Islander peoples there. The people are from many Aboriginal Nations in this area. I was very happy to meet Torres Strait Islander people. I had not known many Torres Strait islanders in my own town. They come from the islands at the top of Queensland. There were lots of children playing and smiling. Some of the Aboriginal languages spoken are Irukandji and Gunggay.

One day during my holiday I visited Yarrabah. I left early from my camp site. It was a long drive. Yarrabah is on the coast below a rainforest mountain. The road is slow and snakes over the mountain. Cassowary live in the rainforest. The people from Yarrabah call these Kindaja (Kin-dah-jah) in their language. They are rare but I spotted one.

When I arrived at Yarrabah I looked around. It is a large community with many houses. It is one of the largest Aboriginal communities in Australia. Many people live here. I found the large arts centre building. A nice local lady welcomed me. She was smiling and asked me about my holiday. She was very kind.

ARTISTS
ALM
Thousands of years of knowledge in the palm of your hand

I asked her if she knows my workmate's family. She quickly said "I'm your friend's aunty". We were both very happy to meet each other. She showed me around the arts centre. I looked at old photos, spears and paintings. I watched some artists as they painted. They were skilful painters. They were very friendly.

I walked around the mission. There were kids playing and swimming. There were horses freely walking around. Horses were eating grass in people's yards. I watched the horses. Horses did not come from Australia. Like many animals now in Australia, they were introduced. That means, they were not here when only Aboriginal people lived in Australia.

Yarrabah sometimes gets cyclones. Cyclones are a very strong storm with lots of wind that can cause lots of damage. The ocean becomes very rough and houses can be damaged. Yarrabah can get cyclones and heavy rains from October to May each year. The houses need to be made strong because of the big storms. During a cyclone the road to Yarrabah can be flooded. People cannot come in or go out until the storm is finished. This can take days. Everyone needs to stay safe.

The sun was going down. The day was nearly over. So I said goodbye to Yarrabah, and the people and horses. I drove back over the mountain. I want to go back and visit again one day. It's a very special place with beautiful nature and friendly people. After a big day I was ready to relax and rest at the campsite again.